Originally published as
My Teacher's in Detention

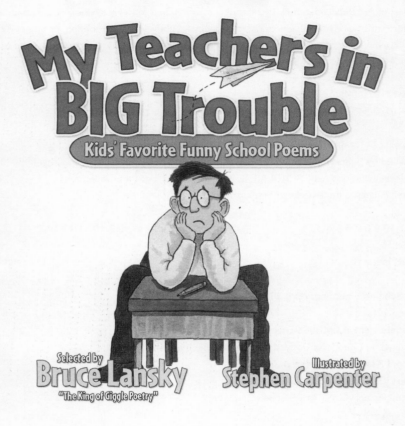

My Teacher's in BIG Trouble

Kids' Favorite Funny School Poems

Selected by
Bruce Lansky
"The King of Giggle Poetry"

Illustrated by
Stephen Carpenter

SCHOLASTIC INC.

New York Toronto London Auckland Sydney
Mexico City New Delhi Hong Kong Buenos Aires

ISBN-13: 978-0-545-09029-2
ISBN-10: 0-545-09029-6

12 11 10 9 8 7 6 5 4 3   8 9 10 11 12 13/0

Printed in the U.S.A.   40

First Scholastic printing, April 2008

Editorial Director: Christine Zuchora-Walske
Coordinating Editor and Copyeditor: Angela Wiechmann
Editorial Assistant: Maureen Burns
Graphic Design Manager: Tamara Peterson
Illustrations and Cover Art: Stephen Carpenter

Acknowledgments

Many thanks to the following teachers and their students
who tested poems for this anthology:

Mark Benthall, Lakeway Elementary, Austin, TX
Cherie Birch, East Elementary, New Richmond, WI
Diane Clapp, Lincoln Elementary, Fairbault, MN
Laura Cook, Lakeway Elementary, Austin, TX
Connie Cooper, Lincoln Elementary, Fairbault, MN
Tara Franke, Deer Creek Elementary, Crowley, TX
Marianne Gately, McCarthy Elementary, Framingham, MA
Pamela Greer, East Elementary, New Richmond, WI
Robin Higgs, W. S. Ryan Elementary, Denton, TX
Sandy Kane, Lincoln Elementary, Fairbault, MN
Kathy Kenney-Marshall, McCarthy Elementary, Framingham, MA
Carolyn Larsen, Rum River Elementary, Andover, MN
Carol Larson, Rum River Elementary, Andover, MN
Carmen Markgren, East Elementary, New Richmond, WI
Maren Morgan-Thomson, District-Topton Elementary, Topton, PA
Jenny Myer, East Elementary, New Richmond, WI
Hope Nadeau, East Elementary, New Richmond, WI
James Parr, McCarthy Elementary, Framingham, MA
John Pundsack, East Elementary, New Richmond, WI
Ruth Refsnider, East Elementary, New Richmond, WI
Cathy Rodrigue, Deer Creek Elementary, Crowley, TX
Connie Roetzer, East Elementary, New Richmond, WI
Andrea Rutkowski, Miscoe Hill School, Mendon, MA
Beverly Semanko, Rum River Elementary, Andover, MN
Maria Smith, Deer Creek Elementary, Crowley, TX
Suzanne Storbeck, Holy Name School, Wayzata, MN
Lisa Thorne, Butler Elementary, Butler, OH
Margaret Weiss, East Elementary, New Richmond, WI
Julie White, Media Specialist, East Elementary, New Richmond, WI

Contents

Introduction

If you enjoyed *No More Homework! No More Tests!* and *If Kids Ruled the School*, you're in for a treat! I just finished reading *My Teacher's in BIG Trouble* before it goes to the printer, and I think you'll love these poems and songs about school.

What I like best are the six songs, and not just because I wrote three of them: "I've Been Sitting in Detention," "The Halls Were Decked," and "Angelica the Beautiful." I'm also crazy about "I've Been Burping in the Classroom" and "My Locker Is Obscene" by Kathy Kenney-Marshall and "Lovely Teacher" by Linda Knaus.

In addition to the funny songs, two of my favorite poems in the book are "The Kindergarten Concert" by Robert Pottle and "Good Morning, Mrs. Hamster" by Kenn Nesbitt. I bet you'll like them, too. And what's not to like about the helpful "rules" you'll find in "Rules for the Bus" by Eric Ode and "The Rules for This Assembly" by Ted Scheu, the Poetry Guy. You'll also learn a lot when you read "What's Inside the Teachers' Lounge?" by Neal Levin. If you've never read "Mrs. Stein" by Bill Dodds, you'll get a big kick out of it. It will thoroughly prepare you for the next time you have a substitute.

As you can tell, I love writing funny poems and songs about school, and I love reading the work of my favorite "giggle poets" and including their very best school poems and songs in my anthologies. I bet *My Teacher's in BIG Trouble* will make you smile. Heck, I bet it'll make you laugh!

Bruce Lansky

Rules for the Bus

Said our driver in September
as we climbed aboard the bus,
"There are rules you must remember.
Number one, you do not cuss.
Do not squirm and do not wiggle.
Do not squeak and do not squawk.
Do not laugh and do not giggle.
Better yet, don't even talk.
Do not ever let me catch you
with your feet out in the aisle.
Sit as rigid as a statue
with a stiff and silent smile.
And you will not wear your mittens,
and you will not wear a mask.
And you will not bring your kittens,
and you shouldn't even ask.
And you will not play with bubbles
or a yo-yo or balloon.
And for causing me such troubles,
you will get them back in June.
Now the day is here. Begin it
with the words I have to say.

2

Kindly take a seat this minute,
and let's have a pleasant day."
Well, I listened very closely
to the messages I heard,
and in all this time I've mostly
followed each and every word.
I have tried to pay attention,
but of this, I must confess:
There's a rule he didn't mention,
and today it caused a mess.
It is not as if I planned it
with an evil attitude.
I am not that underhanded,
and I don't mean to be crude.
But it causes quite a fuss,
and it might even be unlawful
to have climbed aboard the bus
when you have stepped in
    something awful.

Eric Ode

3

Nobody Knows Where Our Bus Driver Goes

Nobody knows
where our bus driver goes
while all of us kids are at school.
Does he study the map?
Does he take a nice nap
or lazily lounge by the pool?

Nobody knows
where our bus driver goes
nor what he may do with his time.
Does he work at the fair?
Is he off cutting hair
or secretly out fighting crime?

Nobody knows
where our bus driver goes.
He's prob'ly a space man from Mars,
but he might be a spy
or a rock 'n' roll guy
who's wailing on 'lectric guitars.

Nobody knows
where our bus driver goes.
He leaves us each morning at eight.
All that we see
is our bus back at three.
And, boy, we're sure glad he's not late!

Jeff Mondak

Peewee Soccer

Christopher is counting clouds.
Hannah braids her hair.
Peter's playing peekaboo.
Greg growls like a bear.

Kevin kicks with all his might,
and though the ball stays put,
his sneaker sails across the field
to land near Roger's foot.

Roger starts to kick the shoe.
Soon poor Kevin's crying.
Katie gives the ball a kick
and sends that ball a-flying.

Billy Brown is looking down.
He sees a four-leaf clover.
Billy wants to pick the plant,
and that's why he bends over.

We see the ball bounce off his bum
and then sail toward the goal.
The goalie gets confused.
We watch him stop then drop and roll.

The other team lets out a cheer
and our team starts to scream
as Billy's bottom scores a goal
for the other team.

Robert Pottle

The Kindergarten Concert

The kindergarten concert was an interesting show.
Peter walked onto the stage and yelled, "I have to go!"
Katie was embarrassed, but she had nowhere to hide.
She raised her dress to hide her face. Her mother almost died.
Keith removed his tie and said, "It's ugly, Dad. I hate it!"
David picked his nose on stage. What's worse is that he ate it.

They sang their song, and Wyatt burped, and then he did a dance.
Michael fell while spinning 'round. Peter wet his pants.
The music teacher at the end said, "There, I'm glad that's done."
The kindergarten bowed and said, "Let's sing another one!"

Robert Pottle

The Field Trip

The bus engine roared as we clambered on board
and took the first seats we could find.
Matthew had thought he'd have time for the bathroom,
but somehow we left him behind.
Pete put a beetle down Eleanor's back.
He just didn't think she would mind.
And Alex threw Tyler's new coat out the window
when Tyler said something unkind.

It rained down a fuss when we got off the bus.
Our teacher was soaked to the skin.
And then when she found she forgot all our lunches,
her patience began to wear thin.
She got so befuddled, she stepped in a puddle.
The water went up to her shin.
And I'd gladly say what she said when it happened,
but I know that swearing's a sin.

We moaned and we groaned as we started back home,
cranky, exhausted, and spent.
Sally was certain her stomach was hurtin'.
We soon understood what she meant.
My teacher might feel that this trip was a failure.
I'm sure that was not her intent.
I'll tell her we had the most wonderful time.
I just can't recall where we went.

Eric Ode

Allergic

I'm allergic to pencils
allergic to ink,
allergic to markers
and crayons, I think.

I'm allergic to homework,
allergic to rules.
To sum it all up:
I'm allergic to schools.

Robert Pottle

Scratch, Scratch, Sniffle

My family has allergies,
all sorts and kinds of strains.
My dad's allergic to our cat.
Mom sniffles when it rains.

My brother can't eat seafood.
He swells right up in lumps.
And sister can't take nature walks,
or she'll break out in bumps.

But as for me, it's pretty odd
what came through our gene pool:
The only time that I get sick
is when I am in school.

Mary Jane Mitchell

My Parents Are Pretending

I'm pretty sure my parents are
pretending they are sick.
I know because I taught them both
to do that little trick.

You blow your nose and hold your head
and claim your brain is breaking.
And so, a pro like me would know
my folks are clearly faking.

A little thing I learned in school
convinced me I am right:
My parents are supposed to meet
my principal tonight.

Ted Scheu

My Locker
Is Obscene

(sing to the tune of "America:
My Country 'Tis of Thee")

My locker is obscene—
worse place you've ever seen.
It's such a mess.
Place where old math tests lie,
old lunch, old apple pie.
The janitor will surely die
when I leave in June.

I'll clean it right away.
I'll throw this stuff away,
like ham and cheese,
bologna green with mold,
thick milk that's four months old,
five chocolate bars I never sold.
I should clean this soon.

I'll start with last month's fruit,
my First Communion suit
from second grade,
three coats, four pairs of shoes,
eight books I'll never use,
pink globs of gum with two more chews,
and an old balloon.

I'm almost halfway through.
Don't know just what to do
with all these ants.
They're crawling everywhere.
There's millions here, I swear.
They're even in old underwear
that I lost last fall.

I think I'm almost done.
I'm sure there's only one
more pile to go.
Five T-shirts almost clean,
my bag from Halloween,
and finally one jellybean.
Whew! I've done it all!

Kathy Kenney-Marshall

Food Fight

We'd never seen the teachers
in a state of such distress.
The principal was yelling
that the lunchroom was a mess.

It started off so innocent
when someone threw a bun,
but all the other kids decided
they should join the fun.

It instantly turned into
an enormous lunchroom feud,
as students started hurling
all their halfway-eaten food.

A glob went whizzing through the air,
impacting on the wall.
Another chunk went sailing out
the doorway to the hall.

18

The food was splattered everywhere—
the ceilings, walls, and doors.
A sloppy, gloppy mess was on
the tables and the floors.

And so our good custodian
ran out to grab his mop.
It took him half the afternoon
to clean up all the slop.

The teachers even used some words
we're not supposed to mention.
And that's how all the kids and teachers
wound up in detention.

Kenn Nesbitt

My Lunch

I didn't like my lunch today
and traded it for Amy's.
She didn't like it either, so
she traded it for Jamie's.
Jamie didn't like it, so
he traded it with Brian.
Brian didn't like it, so
he traded it with Ryan.
Ryan didn't like it, so
he traded it with Jack.
Jack just traded it for mine,
and now I've got it back.

Linda Knaus

Chicken Parts

A picture of a chicken
is in my science book.
Since I am very curious,
I stopped and took a look.

Some arrows pointed to the parts,
like wings and legs and breast.
I saw the beak and feet and tail,
but couldn't find the rest.

I learned a lot about that bird,
but still the question lingers:
Where are all the nuggets
and the patties and the fingers?

Ted Scheu

A Note from Home

Deer Teechur,

Pleeze ekcuze my pore sun Lee—
heeze got the grosist alergee.
Eech time he taykes a speling tesst
it gives him sorze akross his chesst.
The speling kwizz will klog hiz noze
and give him boyills on hiz toze.
Hiz riteing hand will swel and twittch
as all hiz porze beegin to ittch.
So juste to mayke shure heeze ocay,
he shudent tayke the tesst tooday.

Hiz Mom

Robert Scotellaro

Now I Lay Me Down to Rest

Soon I'll lay me down to rest,
but first I have to get undressed,
comb the tangles from my hair,
change my dirty underwear,
have a sandwich and a drink,
clean the plate and rinse the sink,
feed the goldfish, take a bath,
do my spelling and my math,
check my head for ticks and lice,
leave some cheese out for the mice,
fold and put away my pants,
sing a song and do a dance,
say goodnight to Dad and Mother,
pick a fight with my twin brother,
blow my nose and set the clock,
take the dog out for a walk,
turn the light out, pull the shade,
have a glass of lemonade,
trim my toenails, clean my ears,
eat a jar of pickle spears,
kiss Aunt May and Uncle Keith,
wash my face and brush my teeth,
take the garbage to the curb,
learn a pronoun from a verb
so I can pass tomorrow's test—
but now I'm too awake to rest.

Linda Knaus

I've Been Sitting in Detention

(sing to the tune of "I've Been Working on the Railroad")

I've been sitting in detention
since the end of school.
I've been sitting in detention
just because I broke a rule.

Throwing meatballs in the lunchroom
wasn't wise, I fear.
I was aiming at the trash can,
not my teacher's rear.

Teacher let me know
when you'll let me go.
Please don't keep me here all ni-i-ight.
I apologize—
throwing food's not wise.
Don't keep me here all night.

I am going to sneak out of detention
if you will not let me go-o-o-o.
I am going to sneak out of detention,
so, teacher, let me go.

Bruce Lansky

The Halls Were Decked

(sing to the tune of "Deck the Halls")

The halls were decked with toilet paper.
Fa-la-la-la-la, la-la-la-la.
Teacher blamed me for that caper.
Fa-la-la-la-la, la-la-la-la.

Called me names I cannot mention.
Fa-la-la, la-la-la, la-la-la.
Now my teacher's in detention.
Fa-la-la-la-la, la-la-la-la.

Bruce Lansky

Heavy Reading

I have some heavy reading.
My book bag weighs a ton.
It's filled with books I didn't read
and work I haven't done.

But there's no need to worry
'cause everything is cool.
I'll do my homework on the bus
before I get to school.

But first I'll talk to Tommy,
and mess around with Lou.
Are we at school already?
I still have work to do!

I still have time to do it
before the class begins.
But first, a game of tick-tack-toe.
As always, no one wins.

There's the bell! I'm out of time!
I still have not begun!
My science, math, and history—
I'll never get them done!

But just when things seem hopeless,
I hear the teacher say:
"Don't hand your homework in just yet.
I'll give you one more day."

The hours passed. I'm home at last,
and now I'll get it done.
But first, of course, it wouldn't hurt
to have a little fun.

I'll Rollerblade with Billy,
and watch TV with Gus.
Time for bed? My work's not done!
I'll do it on the bus...

Dave Crawley

My Homework

"Hey, Dad, my teacher told me
my homework's really bad.
And if it doesn't soon improve,
then he'll get hopping mad.

"That means I must do better
than I have done before.
So I'm asking you a favor:
Don't help me anymore!"

Bob Woodroffe

What'd You Learn at School Today?

"What'd you learn at school today?"
my mom will surely ask.
I'm certain that my answer
will leave her quite aghast.

I learned that spitwads stick to walls
and on the teacher's cheek.
I learned I have detention
after school for one whole week.

I learned the cafeteria
is a carrot "no-fly" zone.
I learned that I will eat my lunch
in a small room all alone.

I learned that science chemicals
can make a stinking mess.
I learned I lost the privilege
of enjoying noon recess.

I learned my vicious dodge-ball throws
can hurt a person's chin.
I learned that I no longer may
participate in gym.

I learned the school bus is no place
to trip kids with my feet.
I learned that I will ride all year
in a private front-row seat.

If moms would just quit asking,
"What'd you learn at school today?"
their hearts would not be broken
and their hair would not turn gray.

Paul Orshoski

29

I've Been Burping in the Classroom

(sing to the tune of "I've Been Working on the Railroad")

I've been burping in the classroom
since I ate my lunch.
We had beefy, cheesy tacos,
and I gobbled down a bunch.
Can't you hear my belly rumble,
full of greasy taco meat?
Can't you hear the girls all whining,
"Your breath smells like your feet!"

Tacos taste so swell,
but they make you smell.
They're full of beans and spicy me-e-eat!
When you eat a bunch
of that zesty lunch
for sure you won't smell sweet.

Someone needs to tell the lady
when she cooks our lunch today-ay-ay-ay
please leave out the grease and spices
so we can go out and play.

Kathy Kenney-Marshall

31

Vanessa Eats Paste

Vanessa eats paste.
I just saw her chew it.
She must like the taste,
or why would she do it?

She opened the jar
and reached down inside it.
It does seem bizarre,
though I've never tried it.

I asked her if she
was some kind of a nut,
but she couldn't talk
with her jaw pasted shut.

Dave Crawley

PASTE

Snack Time

Crayons are so colorful
but don't have any taste.
Erasers are too chewy.
I don't like eating paste.

Chalk is dry and crunchy.
It always makes me choke.
The frog in the terrarium
would surely make me croak.

Pencils give me splinters.
Pens just make me blue.
The nurse said I'd be punished
the next time I ate glue.

I'm trying something different.
I'm chewing on my comb.
Snack time's always awful
when you leave your snack
   at home.

Robert Pottle

Genie, Please Hurry!

Genie, oh genie, please grant me this wish:
To fly like an eagle, to swim like a fish,
to run like a cheetah, to dart like a snake,
to climb up a mountain or dive in a lake.

Genie, she sees me—there's no time to spare.
She's walking right toward me, she's tossing her hair.
Genie, please hurry and zap me to France
before Callie Johnson can ask me to dance!

Jeff Mondak

It's Finally Friday

It's finally Friday—I'm so glad.
It's been a crazy week.
I got chewed out on Monday,
and since then it's all been bleak.

I lost my lunch on Tuesday,
and a parent went insane,
which shocked me so completely
that I almost popped a vein.

I poked my eye on Wednesday,
and the nurse gave me a shot.
She sent me to the doctor
when I fainted on the spot.

On Thursday I was tardy
'cause I kinda overslept.
And the snack that I was craving
came up missing in a theft.

And so it's finally Friday.
No more pencils, no more books.
No more sitting in detention,
no more teachers' dirty looks.

By Friday I'm exhausted,
out of energy and breath.
But that's the day you'll hear me shout,
"Rejoice, TGIF!"

And twice a month on Friday,
I remember why I stay:
You see, I am the principal—
that's when I get my pay.

Paul Orshoski

Mrs. Stein

The school bell rings; we go inside.
Our teacher isn't there.
"Maybe she's sick!" her pet cries out.
Yeah, right. As if I'd care.

I have a D in language arts.
My grade in math's the same.
And now my teacher might be sick—
could be I'm part to blame.

She doesn't like me, that's a fact.
I wouldn't tell a lie.
She says stuff like, "You're very smart,
but you don't even try."

I start to laugh—my teacher's sick!
And, boy, I'm feeling fine...
Then someone kicks the door right in,
and there stands Frankenstein.

She's six foot eight, her dress is black,
she's wearing combat boots.
I start to gasp. She growls and says,
"I'll be your substitute."

The teacher's pet is whimpering;
she doesn't stand a chance.
The smart kid stares and points and faints.
The bully wets his pants.

"My name is Mrs. Stein," she says,
and every student cringes.
She leans the door against the wall—
she'd knocked it off its hinges.

"Now let's begin. You there! Stand up!"
She looks me in the eye.
I try to move, my legs won't work.
I know I'm going to die!

In one big step she's next to me,
and she does more than hover.
She blocks the sun, it's dark as night.
My classmates run for cover.

"Now get up to the board," she says.
"I'd like to see some action.
Pick up the chalk, explain to us
division of a fraction."

I leap away to save my life.
This time I *really* try.
I think and think and think and croak,
"Invert and multiply."

"Correct!" she says. I breathe again
and head back for my chair.
"You, FREEZE," she shouts,
 and I stop cold,
"and don't go anywhere."

This all begins at nine o'clock.
I fight to stay alive.
It seems to last a million years—
the clock says nine-o-five.

That's just three hundred seconds,
and then my turn is through.
She points at every one of us.
"Now, you. Now, you. Now, you."

We all get nailed this awful day.
There's nowhere we can hide.
The lunch bell rings, we cannot eat.
We simply crawl outside.

We can't believe the other kids
who run and play their games.
Not us, who have big Mrs. Stein.
Our world is not the same.

The bell has tolled, I must go in.
My time on earth is through.
I'll leave this on the playground—
here's what you have to do:

You must listen to your teacher
and pray her health is fine,
or one day soon you'll hear the words,
"My name is Mrs. Stein."

Bill Dodds

41

The Rules for This Assembly
(As Explained by Our Very Silly Principal)

"Raise your hand
if you're not here.
Do it now,
sometime next year.

"Please don't move,
except to wiggle.
Do not laugh,
except to giggle.

"Sit up tall
so you can't see.
Buy a ticket,
they are free.

"Close your mouth
and say hello.
Quickly do it,
very slow.

"Let's all cry
and have some fun.
We'll start as soon
as we are done."

Ted Scheu

My Teacher Loves Her iPod

My teacher loves her iPod.
It's always in her ear.
She doesn't mind it if we joke
or chat 'cause she can't hear.

If we don't pay attention,
she doesn't seem to care.
Whenever she has music on,
she wears a distant stare.

Our principal dropped by one day,
and she paid no attention.
He took away her iPod,
and he sent her to detention.

Bruce Lansky

What's Inside the Teachers' Lounge?

What's inside the teachers' lounge?
I'd really like to know.
I bet it's eighty-five degrees.
Our classroom's ten below.

I think they have a microwave
for pizza by the slice,
and soda pop in one machine,
another full of ice.

There's probably a TV set
that has a giant screen
and beanbag chairs and lava lamps,
perhaps a putting green.

I'd have to guess the teachers' lounge
has all the coolest features.
The only things that ruin it
are all those doggone teachers.

Neal Levin

Angelica the Beautiful

(sing to the tune of "America the Beautiful")

Angelica's so beautiful,
her teeth are pearly white.
And when she smiles, I turn to mush.
She's such a stunning sight.
It's true I have a crush on her,
of that there is no doubt.
That's why I tease her every day—
so no one will find out.

One day when we walked home from school,
she slipped her hand in mine.
I thought that she was sending me
a clear romantic sign.
I smiled and gave her cheek a kiss
to prove my love was true.
That's when she gave my face a slap,
so now it's black-and-blue.

Bruce Lansky

46

That Girl

That girl from Mrs. Finster's room
is coming down the hall.
I'd hide inside a locker,
but I think that I'm too tall.
That girl is coming closer still.
She'll see me soon, I fear.
If I knew how, you bet that
I'd completely disappear.
She's almost right in front of me.
She looks straight in my eye.
I'm catching claustrophobia.
I think I just might die.
And then she stops and kicks my leg.
I hold my wounded knee.
I'm thankful that I know at last
that girl's in love with me!

Kathy Kenney-Marshall

47

My Class Has Got a Know-It-All

My class has got a know-it-all—
the kind who likes to tell
the proper way to sit and walk
and count and speak and spell.

My class has got a know-it-all—
the kind who always knows
the stuff that happened yesterdays
or even long agos.

She's constantly correcting me
if I'm a little wrong,
like when I bring a bug to class
or when I sing a song.

You might think I'd be angry with
this showy, knowy creature.
But someday I will be like her:
I'm going to be a teacher.

Ted Scheu

Ooh! Ooh! I Know!

The teacher called on Jonathan—
I had my hand up first.
He couldn't even answer "What's
the opposite of *worst*?"

My arm is getting sore 'cause, like,
I've kept it up so long,
and yet she called on Bethany,
who got the next one wrong.

Oh please! This stuff's so easy! Betcha
I could teach this class.
(And Kyle, "The Stinker," should
    have known
that methane is a gas.)

Hello? You might try picking *me*.
It's just a small suggestion.
"Uh, yes ma'am?...Me?...Oh
    gosh...What's that?
I didn't hear the question."

Christopher Cook

49

Good Morning, Mrs. Hamster

The teacher performed an experiment
she probably shouldn't have tried.
Some chemicals flashed and exploded.
She ended up frazzled and fried.

Her eyebrows were sizzling and smoking.
Her clothing was covered with soot.
She looked like a cartoon coyote
whose cannon had just gone kaput.

But something astonishing happened
as soon as her test went awry.
The teacher was caught by the shock wave,
and so was her hamster nearby.

The universe inside the blast zone
was literally rearranged,
affecting the teacher and hamster,
and somehow their brains were exchanged.

The hamster climbed up near the blackboard
and handed out homework galore.
The teacher, by contrast, was squeaking
and crawling around on the floor.

The principal quickly came running
the instant he learned of the news.
The hamster said, "Welcome. Please join us."
Our teacher was sniffing his shoes.

I'm sorry to say our poor teacher
now sits in a cage eating grass.
The principal says she's our pet now.
The hamster's in charge of the class.

Kenn Nesbitt

Perfect

Today I managed something
that I've never done before:
I turned in this week's spelling quiz
and got a perfect score.
Although my score was perfect,
it appears I'm not too bright.
I got a perfect zero—
not a single answer right.

Kenn Nesbitt

TEST

53

Today I Had a Rotten Day

Today I had a rotten day
as I was coming in from play.
I accidentally stubbed my toes
and tripped and fell and whacked my nose.

I chipped a tooth. I cut my lip.
I scraped my knee. I hurt my hip.
I pulled my shoulder, tweaked my ear,
and got a bruise upon on my rear.

I banged my elbow, barked my shin.
A welt is forming on my chin.
My pencil poked me in the thigh.
I got an eyelash in my eye.

I sprained my back. I wrenched my neck.
I'm feeling like a total wreck.
So that's the last time I refuse
when teacher says to tie my shoes.

Kenn Nesbitt

Another Note from Mom

I sprang from bed and bumped my head and stubbed my little toe,
then jammed my fingers turning down the blaring radio.

I rubbed my bumps and bruises as the weather lady said,
"Today's the first of April, look for showers overhead."

I trudged downstairs to breakfast, where my bad luck tagged along.
There taped up to the microwave...another note from Mom:

Good morning! Exclamation point—she always starts out nice.
Now comes the part where I get fed her motherly advice.

*For breakfast, dear, just help yourself. There's pizza in the fridge.
And as for soda, choose the Sprite— the Coke has lost its fizz.*

"Is this a dream?" I said out loud. "There must be some mistake.
I'd better read that through again. I'm only half awake."

I scanned the lines, not once, but twice. Yes, *pizza's* what it said!
And I could swallow that advice, so I read on ahead:

Please wear your faded jeans to school, those low-cut ones that flare.
And use my mousse to do that sticky-up thing with your hair.

"Is she for real?" I asked myself. "What's gotten into Mom?"
Whatever it was, I liked it lots, so I continued on:

About your science quiz today—the one on natural gas—
just tell your teacher that's one subject you don't want to pass!

I know I didn't read that right. I couldn't have, no way!
But there it was in black and white, as plain as night and day.

And then it hit me, why the change: Mom hadn't lost a screw;
my worry-free philosophy had finally gotten through.

Her rules had changed from lame to lax—my mom was cool at last!
These last few months of middle school were gonna be a blast!

I quickly read the last few lines: *Enjoy your day at school!*
(And don't believe what you've just read—or you're an April Fool!)

Diane Z. Shore

A Work of Art

I followed her directions.
I did what she had said.
I painted with my paintbrush
and used the color red.

I drew with magic markers
and made a nice design.
I took my wooden chisel
and carved a perfect line.

Before the class was over,
I showed her what I did.
When I saw her reaction,
I almost ran and hid.

I followed her directions!
I thought I'd get a star!
Instead I got detention
for my artwork on her car.

Darren Sardelli

My Teacher Sees Right Through Me

I didn't do my homework.
My teacher asked me, "Why?"
I answered him, "It's much too hard."
He said, "You didn't try."

I told him, "My dog ate it."
He said, "You have no dog."
I said, "I went out running."
He said, "You never jog."

I told him, "I had chores to do."
He said, "You watched TV."
I said, "I saw the doctor."
He said, "You were with me."

My teacher sees right through my fibs,
which makes me very sad.
It's hard to fool your teacher
when your teacher is your dad.

— Bruce Lansky

59

Lovely Teacher
(sing to the tune of "Clementine")

Lovely teacher, lovely teacher—
eyes of periwinkle blue.
You are such a pretty creature,
and I'm so in love with you.

How I long for your attention,
so I'm acting like a fool.
Put me down for some detention,
just don't send me home from school.

Oh, I'm filled with pain and sorrow,
for my teacher is so cute,
but she won't be here tomorrow,
'cause she's just a substitute.

Linda Knaus

Afterschool Snack

Right now I'm kinda hungry, dude.
The 'frigerator's full of food.
There's meat loaf and a chicken wing
and half a turkey sandwich-thing.

There's day-old tuna, almost new,
some Tupperware with potluck stew,
some leftover spaghetti sauce,
and wilted salad partly tossed.

There's also Jell-O (sort of green),
a chunk of cheese, a lima bean,
a jar of pickles, can of soup,
and something best described as goop.

There's broccoli that's growing old,
a loaf of bread that's growing mold...
The 'frigerator's full, but hey—
there's nothing that I want today.

Neal Levin

61

I Brought My Grandma's Teeth to School

I brought my grandma's teeth to school to share for show-and-tell.
Billy showed his sneakers. It was more like show-and-*smell*.
Kevin brought a violin and showed he couldn't play.
Katie brought her snake to school—too bad it got away.
Our class likes show-and-tell a lot, so we were sad to hear
our teacher say that show-and-tell is canceled till next year.

Robert Pottle

Looking for Poems

My teacher said I had to read a poem aloud in class.
I looked and could not find one, and I'm running out of gas!
I looked inside my drawer, but all I found was underwear.
I slammed my pinkie in the drawer, and Mommy heard me swear.
She made me go to bed at six; she made me suck on soap,
which made me feel so grumpy that I called my mom a dope.
So then I had to stay inside the whole next Saturday.
I couldn't ride my bike or go outside to run and play.
And so I tried to find that poem my teacher asked me for.
I looked inside my toy box and behind the closet door.
I looked beneath the dresser, and I crawled beneath my bed.
I found no poems, then crawled back out and badly bumped my head.
I stubbed my toe, and then I made my problems even worse:
My mom walked in and heard me as I accidentally cursed!
Again I had to suck on soap and then go straight to bed.
But still no stupid poem for school—I might stay home instead.
I lay down on the floor and sulked, then drifted off to sleep,
when all at once into my brain a poem began to creep.
It snuck into my sleepy brain and played with me a while.
When I woke up I wrote a poem that made me really smile.
And later on, I realized as I lay upon my bed:
The bestest place to find a poem is right inside my head!

Kathy Kenney-Marshall

My Doggy Ate My Essay

My doggy ate my essay,
he picked up all my mail.
He cleaned my dirty closet,
and he dusted with his tail.

He straightened out my posters
and swept my wooden floor.
My parents almost fainted
when he fixed my bedroom door.

I did not try to stop him.
He made my windows shine.
My room looked like a palace,
and my dresser smelled like pine.

He fluffed up every pillow.
He folded all my clothes.
He even cleaned my fish tank
with a toothbrush and a hose.

I thought it was amazing
to see him use a broom.
I'm glad he ate my essay
on "How to Clean My Room."

Darren Sardelli

66

Parent-Teacher Conference

At the parent-teacher conference,
my father made a scene.
He scared my fifth-grade teacher
with his mask from Halloween.

She showed him all my science grades
and said she was concerned,
but he just stuck his tongue out
when my teacher's back was turned.

He drew a monster on the board
and claimed it was her twin.
He even shook her soda,
which exploded on her chin.

My angry teacher crossed her arms
and said, "This meeting's done!
I now see where he gets it from—
you act just like your son!"

Darren Sardelli

Credits

Author Index

Title Index